The Purposeful Personal Brand

You, Now and in the Future

Michael E. Piperno

DEDICATION

To all who have encouraged me to trust my instincts.

I am grateful for you.

Especially you, Joe.

CONTENTS

ACKNOWLEDGMENTS

This book and my career have been shaped and nurtured by many people for whom I will always be grateful.

Special thanks to David Esposito, Patty Lavigne, Ken Maisel, Cathleen McNulty, Michael Morris, Lisa Peluso, Mara Connolly Taft, and Pete Taft.

CHAPTER 1

WHEN PURPOSE LEADS

Amid the aromatic blend of coffee, split pea soup and gym socks, this study hall is quiet, with just the low murmur of teenagers planning their next adventure.

Red pen in hand, I grade quizzes while keeping an eye on the students seated at a cafeteria table a few yards away.

Yesterday at this time I was breaking up a fight and got punched in the face while doing so. The student didn't mean to punch me, but my face got in the way as I tried to stop her from seriously injuring the girl she was beating. Later that afternoon, the mother of the girl who hit me called me and told me she would "rip me a new asshole" if I ever interfered in her daughter's affairs again.

I look around the room and realized, "I can't do this until I'm 67."

Yes, I had just spent four and a half years in a career I was going to leave behind — one month before I was to receive tenure, which would bring the kind of job security that was increasingly becoming uncommon. Was I crazy?

I thought I was *sure* I wanted to be a teacher. Well, that was after realizing that being an actor wasn't right for me. I wanted to help people, like so many teachers who had helped me.

And I adored my students (mostly). What was the problem? I won't go into all the factors that informed my decision to leave, but let's just say there were enough reasons that I knew I wanted out.

26 years old and completely lost. Like a failure — that's how I felt. Everyone around me was disappointed. I was leaving a secure job that was very hard to come by during those times. I looked foolish

THE PURPOSEFUL PERSONAL BRAND

in the eyes of many, and in turn, felt foolish—thought my gut was telling me otherwise.

Those feelings were wrong.

In fact, I was courageous. I was experiencing the effects of a misaligned purpose on my day-to-day work life. I didn't know it then, but I was not willing to allow the expectations of other people to dictate what I did with my career. I was letting my purpose lead the way, even if I didn't really know where I was going.

I got a hybrid job as a project manager and part-time graphic designer for a financial services firm. The woman who hired me took a chance on me.

I loved that job.

24 years later, I'm a leadership communication coach and trainer, and a career transition expert. I also teach at a local university. In between my days as a high school teacher and now, I've been a marketing manager, account manager, graphic designer, public

speaking professor, creative director, small business owner, and brand agency leader.

Sounds like a wandering path, right?

It's not. I'll explain later.

CHAPTER 2

LOOKING IN THE MIRROR

When you look at your professional self in the mirror, who do you see?

How do you describe yourself?

Are you happy with who you see?

There have been times during my career where I have answered that last question with an emphatic, "Yes!"

There have also been several times where I have said, "No, no, no, no, no. Definitely not." Just like that day in the high school cafeteria.

As someone who has put a lot of deeply personal work into his career, those times were pretty hard for me.

When I look in the mirror, I see a good guy who appears outgoing, but is a classic introvert when you really get to know him. Most people describe him as friendly and talented, and a very hard worker although he always thinks he should be doing more.

People also describe him as confident. He guesses that's partly due to his work ethic and the fact that he isn't afraid to stand up in front of others and teach or present. Or maybe it's because he is an entrepreneur.

The truth is that he often doubts his talents and accomplishments. Actually, at times he even fears being exposed as a fraud after taking a risk, even though he is clear with himself that everything he does for others is done with the intent to help.

His professional past reads like mishmash of different jobs and career paths without much of a logical progression. No obvious climbing of the corporate ladder at any one company. No mega "wins" that have made him a millionaire.

And he used to let the opinions of others affect his

view of himself.

Ugh. I'm really laying it all out on the table for you. But it's important that I do so.

Until a few years ago, I struggled to express my passions, value, and purpose clearly. After years of frustration reading books and attending workshops trying to figure out how to get to the heart of who I am and what I want to do when I grow up (a funny thing to say at my age), I got fed up and created my own system for finding happiness and fulfillment.

My system is described in detail in chapters 3 through 7 of this book. And I'm sharing it with you because, as you will see, I want others to pursue their purpose as fiercely as I do.

The *Purposeful Personal Brand* process described in these pages has helped me find my purpose and tell my story in a way that nobody looking at a typical résumé or CV would ever see.

This process helped me find the common thread in my career ambitions — the stuff that makes me tick. The passion that makes me want to work, to create, and to inspire others....

When I found my purpose and was *finally* able to articulate it clearly to myself and to others, I saw clearly how every position, every decision, and every single step I have made during my career has been true to my purpose (well, mostly).

As you know, our purpose is what makes work most meaningful to us. For me, pursuing it has meant taking risks, but I've calculated them carefully, never putting my well-being or my family in too much danger (there's been a little). And because I now have a stronger sense of purpose, I find that I get myself unstuck faster than other people I know.

To some that makes me look like a risk taker. To me, it's the opposite.

To me, it's simply necessary. I can't be authentically me without it.

CHAPTER 3

PERSONAL BRAND DISCOVERY

In the next few chapters, I am going to share the foundational elements of my personal brand discovery process that I use for myself and my clients. It focuses on finding your purpose and then working to make sure you can communicate it to yourself and to others.

When you get comfortable doing so your personal brand becomes much more powerful. And the bonus is that it also becomes more portable. Why is portability important?

Because how we traditionally think of our

personal brand working for us is wrong.

Much like a pension or corporate health benefits, our personal brands are often tied to who we're working *for*. So, we tend to mold it to fit *them*, instead of serving *ourselves*.

Think about that for a second.

We look for jobs, opportunities, or even clients who need something from us. They need us to produce, manage, and problem solve—right?

Here's what I believe. We should be looking for jobs, opportunities, and clients who *want or need what we do best*—and who are at least somewhat aligned with our passions. Then we can be truly purposeful in helping them.

And guess what? This will make you virtually future-proof. You'll be able to *pivot* more easily than most.

What Exactly is a Personal Brand?

People often think of a personal brand as something you create to market yourself, like a product. That's part of it, but I define it much more deeply. For me it's the essence of who you are — your passions, what you value, the value you bring to others, and your authentic purpose — and yes, ultimately how you choose to show it to the world.

But remember that nobody is perfect.

Like the most beautiful diamond you've ever seen, it still has flaws. You're the same. I'm the same. We all are. However, we have a choice, every day, of which facets of our diamond to show to which people. The trick is figuring out how to do this in a way that feels authentic and true to who you are. Knowing our purpose helps.

Also remember that nobody's path or story is straightforward. One of the only things we can guarantee in life is that **things will change**.

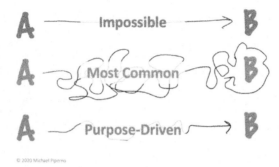

A clear easy path in our professional lives is simply not typical. And if you are on a simple path, you're likely bored. If you're on a haphazard path, it can feel confusing or overwhelming.

When you find your purpose, you have a guide that keeps your eye on the *right path*, even as the path changes.

CHAPTER 4

FINDING YOUR PURPOSE

Many people have not taken the time to think deeply about their passions, value, and purpose. In work *or* in life.

Let's fix that. Today. Right now.

Warning: Read this chapter and complete its activities when you have at least 60 minutes of **uninterrupted time**.

That's right — turn your smartphone off or put it in Do Not Disturb mode!

You in 3 Parts

In the following pages are several prompts and questions that will help you become clearer about your passions, value, and purpose.

Don't write your answers down yet. You'll do so after you're read parts 1, 2, and 3 of the process.

Part 1: First, you'll think about yourself in general and complete the following sentences.

- I am...
- I am *not*...
- I am passionate about...
- I am good at...
- My personal goals are...
- My professional goals are...

Part 2: Next, you'll think about your value and differentiators, especially when it comes to work. So, keep your ideal client or job position in mind — even if you're not 100% sure who or what that is yet.

- Who is my audience(s)?

- What problems do I solve for them?

- What gives me credibility with them?

- What value do I bring to them through my work?

- What results will I create for them?

- How do I want them to describe me to their friends, family, and colleagues?

Part 3: Finally, you'll look for common themes and make a list of them. Note that the common themes don't always jump right out at you. You may need to step back and take some time to think about what you wrote in parts 1 and 2 before the common themes or threads will emerge.

I have provided an example for you in the back of this book. It's how I answered parts 1 through 3. However, I prefer you try yours first — I don't want my answers to influence you.

Your turn!

Answer each question in the following pages openly and honestly. There are no wrong answers. If you are confused by any of the questions or don't know what to write, just do your best.

Oh, and write as much as you can. The more you put into this exercise, the better you'll be able to begin to see the story you should be telling yourself, and your audiences.

Part 1: Describe Yourself

Complete the following sentences in this book, or on a separate sheet of paper. You can write more than one thing for each sentence.

I am...

I am not...

I am passionate about…

I am good at…

My personal goals are…

My professional goals are…

Good job! Review your answers above one more time and make any edits or additions.

Part 2: Describe Your Value and Your Differentiators

As you complete this section, keep your ideal client or job in mind — even if you're not 100% sure who or what that is yet.

Who is my audience(s)?

What problems do, or can I, solve for them?

What gives me credibility with them?

What value do I bring to them through my work?

What results will I create for them?

How do I want them to describe me to their friends, family, and colleagues?

Part 3: Common Themes or Threads

Review parts 1 and 2 and look for common themes a make a list of them. Note that the common themes don't always jump right out at you. You may need to step back and take some time to think about it. That's okay.

List your common themes here. What's emerging? What are you seeing, or thinking?

If a clear theme or tread is not becoming clear to you, take some time to think through your responses. You can even do parts 1 and 2 of the exercise again. Once you begin to notice themes that feel good to you, try to write a purpose statement for yourself. Read on....

Your Purpose Statement

This statement is not something you'll share with others. It is meant to help you solidify your purpose in your yeat, try to write a purpose statement anyway. You can always revise it later.

Here's a first draft of mine:

> *To use my passion for teaching and my communication expertise to help people — to build them up so they can better leverage their talents, experience, and authentic selves to crush their goals (and feel more fulfilled while doing so).*

Will I revise that statement over time? Sure. But the essence is there. And you know what? It's so true to who I am that I can even look back at little 15-year-old me and say, "Yup — he was the same back then."

I knew I loved to help others and "be on the stage." I thought it meant being an actor or teacher of some kind but didn't know what kind. And I got it wrong in the beginning of my career.

But I found it, as a 40-something adult using the tools I just showed you.

Not sure about your statement yet? Review your work from this chapter. Think about who you are, what you want to do, and why you want to do it.

These questions might help:

- Who am I at my core?
- What do I do (or want to do)?
- Why do I want to do it?
- Who do I do it for?
- How do I make a difference for them? How are they changed?
- How do I want to be remembered?

Here's how I answered those questions:

Who am I at my core?	I am a teacher, trainer, mentor, and coach.
What do I do (or want to do)?	Help people be better communicators. Improve how people communicate at work so they can be more effective.
Why do I want to do it?	Because nothing fulfils me more than helping others be their best selves. I like playing a role in the success of others. And I believe that communication is the key to solving most problems.
Who do I help?	Leaders, emerging leaders, teams, and entrepreneurs.
How are they changed?	They become more self-aware of their superpowers and blind spots, and of the same in others. Better relationships, more satisfaction, better results.
How do I want to be remembered?	As someone who was trusted to help, and who played a role in making life better and more fulfilling for others.

And here is my shortened version of my purpose statement after a little more reflection:

I use my passion for teaching and expertise in communications to help people lead, and be their best at work.

28

Write your purpose statement here:

To help you be your best for those you care about most at Home, at Work, and in the Community

Once you feel fairly confident with your purpose and the value you bring to the people you can help, read on to learn how to tell your story with maximum impact.

CHAPTER 5

PERSONAL STORYTELLING

In business, everyone has a story to tell. In this context, I'm not talking about fairy tales or fictional stories that are simply meant to entertain. I'm talking about crafting a narrative that showcases your unique strengths, talents, and value.

I've thought about this topic a lot over the years. Why is it so hard for many people to tell their own stories? And what happens when talented people don't do it well? There's an interesting Ted talk by Carla Harris[1] where she talks about finding people who can help you get ahead at work — and she makes some powerful points about how many people who are good at what they do have not put enough work into telling their stories or into relationship building. Therefore, there's nobody else fighting for them. I'll let you watch the talk to find out what her solution is, but it made me think about a lot of brilliant, talented, and wonderful people I have known during my career who let other people control their narratives.

Many people think of personal storytelling, or even personal branding, as shameless promotion. That's often because the people they've seen do it have been the types who happily talk about themselves while speaking over others in the room. It doesn't have to be like that. In fact, it shouldn't be like that at all.

Think of storytelling as a guide—one that carefully leads others along the path to understanding, and remembering, you. Whether you're an introvert or extrovert, talkative or quiet, passive or assertive, you can find a comfortable way to talk about yourself that showcases the right parts of you to the right people. Then, you can build stronger connections and relationships, and be remembered.

You're a Diamond

In a past episode of Dave Stachowiak's excellent podcast Coaching for Leaders,[2] he interviewed leadership and entrepreneurship expert and professor Laura Huang about her book, Edge: Turning Adversity into Advantage. On the podcast, Laura shared this wonderful visual of how we show ourselves to others. She said to think of yourself as a diamond. Every diamond has flaws. And every diamond has many beautiful, and different, facets.

There's great power in learning to show the right facets to the right people. You're not being inauthentic by doing so. It's still you, but you're tailoring the story to the audience to ensure you are guiding them in better understanding the aspects of you *that matter to them*.

Whether you're trying to climb the corporate ladder, sell a product or service, or launch your own business, it's easier to influence others when your communication considers the needs of your audience and is tailored to tell them the story that they need to hear.

And most importantly, make sure you're in control of your story.

CHAPTER 6

CRAFTING A STORY THAT CONNECTS

I hope you are feeling energized and ready to take the next steps in crafting a story for your purposeful personal brand—one that connects with other people.

I'm sure you can see that when it comes to your personal brand, simply "being yourself" isn't enough. You need to tell your story clearly and confidently. And yes, that does require a little persuasion and influence—but only the ethical and authentic kind.

You're not being inauthentic by doing so. It's still you, but you're tailoring the story to the audience to ensure you are guiding them in better understanding the aspects of you that matter to them.

If you don't help them by telling a clear story, you leave it up to them to craft their own story about you. That's how talented people get overlooked at work, and how entrepreneurs miss opportunities to build their audiences.

Telling Your Story the Right Way to the Right People

Knowing your audience is the first rule of communication. Once you've considered them, then you can craft a story that is true to you yet tailored to them. Make sense?

Think about one or two stakeholders who you need to inspire or show yourself to with clarity and confidence. Complete the exercise below for each — it will give you a good foundation for how you need to tailor your story for others in the future.

Stakeholder 1 Name: _____

My diamond facets that apply to this
stakeholder or situation (Strengths,
Expertise, Passions, Purpose, Value,
Differentiation…):

Top 3 to 5 facets from the list above that
you want to ensure are noticed by this
stakeholder:

Stakeholder 2 Name: _____

My diamond facets that apply to this stakeholder or situation (Strengths, Expertise, Passions, Purpose, Value, Differentiation…):

Top 3 to 5 facets from the list above that you want to ensure are noticed by this stakeholder:

Good. Now you can tailor the story to what *they need to hear*—showing them the facets that really matter and will connect with them. Read on to see how to do just that.

CHAPTER 7

TELLING YOUR STORY

I've probably written or refined more than 200 elevator pitches over the years—you know, the short blurb that you're supposed to memorize and be ready to spew out in the time that it takes to impress a prospect during an elevator ride.

Elevator Pitches are Boring

The concept behind the elevator pitch makes sense. You need to be able to tell someone about your product, service, or organization quickly and clearly. And yes, you need to be prepared to do so.

However, when you stop thinking about "pitching" and start thinking of it as sharing or educating, you can turn a dry, planned pitch into something much more useful: a conversation.

Here's how to do it:

1. Think about your audiences—who you help and how you help them, or how the person you're speaking with might be able to help you if they know the right people. Then write down several short statements about how you solve their problems, make a difference, or what you see as your best fit for your next chapter. These will become what I call your "library of nuggets." Some examples (these are 4 different people, yours will be all about you):

    1. "I help people overcome their fear of public speaking."

    2. "I make complex data easier to grasp for non-analytical people."

    3. "My work has been featured in the industry's top journal."

4. My expertise lends itself best to medical diagnostics.

If you're marketing a product or service in these conversations, be sure to include a few nuggets about why your solutions or abilities are unique or better than others.

2. When you meet someone new or have an interaction with a key stakeholder, try to get them talking first. This will not only make you more approachable (you're showing them that you care about who they are and what they do), it will also allow you to steer the conversation in a way where you can connect with them and start a meaningful conversation.

3. Once you have engaged them in a conversation (instead of a pitch), pull from your library of nuggets to tailor your conversation to their specific perspective and needs.

Try to start with a question that you think they will be able to answer easily, which will let you include them in the story you're about to tell.

Here's an example:

Hi, I'm Thomas. What's your name?

I'm Dana.

Nice to met you, Dana. What do you do?

I'm in human resources. How about you?

Well, in HR I'm sure you know see how challenging it is for your senior leaders to communicate well when they deal with so many different personalities in the company.

Yes, it's a problem. We've actually lost some top talent because their managers were poor communicators.

That happens in almost every company. The problem is that it's often too late to fix when the top talent is already checked out. I develop coaching and training programs to give leaders the skills they need to prevent communication breakdowns and build cultures that keep top talent.

I think you should come in and talk to my HR leadership team.

And here's another example:

Hi, I'm Diandre.

Hi, I'm Andrew. What area of the company do you work in?

I'm in marketing. Are you familiar with the marketing programs we run at our company?

Not really. I lead the regulatory function here. I don't know much about our marketing programs, except the ads I see on the internet and social media. I do hear we do a good job attracting customers through your efforts.

Thanks! I track the performance of those ads you see. In fact, that's the piece of the marketing mix that I am most passionate about — analytics. If people don't measure our efforts well, it's impossible to understand what's working and what's not. That can lead to poor performance and wasted money.

I'm glad we have people like you here who can promote our business effectively and track performance of all the different efforts. I could never do that — my brain is wired differently.

It is complicated. But for me, it's fascinating at the same time. It's also rewarding to be able to report to my team which campaigns are working especially well. And when we see one that's not working, we can get insights from the data I track to help adjust the campaign. Hey, I'm sure things in the world of regulatory can be quite complex, too. Right?

Yes, for sure — but in a different way than the work you do. What I have to watch out for is....

And one final example:

Hi, I'm Margo.

Hi, I'm Arun. It's nice to meet you.

Yes, it's nice to meet you, too. How are you enjoying this networking event? Are you connecting with the types of people who can help you?

Not many, but that's typical, right? I'm having some nice conversations though. Always good to meet new people. You never know who's going to know somebody who can be a good connection. How about you?

A few. I've had a great run in big pharma, and now I'm ready to use my skills and experience to help lead an early-stage company. I'm particularly excited about companies doing innovative work in the diagnostics space. The people who can help me most are founders of small biotech companies who are looking for a leader to help them build a team and raise money, or venture capitalists who want to help one of their companies build a leadership team and scale the business.

My brother-in-law heads up a VC firm. I'm pretty sure biotech and life sciences make up a lot of their investments.

Give me your information and I'll see if he wants to speak with you.

Do you see how a real conversation helps the other person get to know you, and hear your passions, value, and purpose?

Not every conversation will be the same, and that's the point. An elevator pitch is written for one person, you. Real connections require more.

Whether you are speaking with a senior leader at your company, a new prosect for your business, or someone you casually meet at a networking function, give them the courtesy of a conversation.

Just be ready with your *library of nuggets* so you feel prepared to tailor the conversation for each individual.

Use the space below to create a library of nuggets for yourself. Try to come up with at least 10 nuggets.

Once you're done, test yourself by practicing

pulling from your library and telling a few friends or colleagues who you are and what you do. **Practice makes ~~perfect~~ experts**™ (perfection doesn't exist).

Your Library of Nuggets

CHAPTER 8

NEXT STEPS

You did it! The work you've done while reading this book has formed the foundation for your purposeful personal brand.

Now you need to grow it.

Look back over the exercises from this book and refine anything that needs additional reflection or clarification. Then, start talking to others about your passions, value, and purpose. The more you practice speaking with different people about who you are and how you help, the easier it will be to tell your story comfortably and confidently—in a way that will matter to every listener.

An Ongoing Process

Never let your personal brand stagnate. Allow your purpose to evolve and grow. I go through the exercises from this book at least once per year. And when I am feeling a little lost or unfocused, I do it more often.

You can find a schedule that works for you but revisiting this exercise and fine tuning on a regular basis will keep your passions, value, and purpose top of mind.

Then it will remain *portable*. That means you'll always be ready to adapt when needed, whether for a new product or service line, a new position, or even a new career.

I'm cheering for you.

PERSONAL BRAND DISCOVERY EXAMPLE

To help you see how this works, I'm going to detail my responses for parts 1 through 3 from Chapter 3.

Please try to do this exercise on your own before reviewing my answers!

Part 1: About Me

- I am...
    - Kind
    - A teacher
    - Competitive (with myself, and not~~e~~) ✓ with others)
    - Empathetic (sometimes to a fault)
    - Confident (mostly)
    - An introvert who is comfortable being an extrovert when needed
    - Thoughtful
    - Fun (I think)
    - A risk taker (when calculated)
- I am not...

- o A good networker
  - o A marketing "doer" (but I do give good advice)
  - o Sales-y
  - o Tolerant of meanness
- I am passionate about…
  - o Helping others unleash the power within themselves
  - o Family and true friends
  - o The arts
  - o The power of thoughtful and clear communication
- I am good at…
  - o Listening
  - o Teaching
  - o Speaking in public
  - o Empathizing
  - o Guiding people who feel lost in their careers
  - o Technology
  - o Communicating
- My personal goals are…
  - o Provide for my family now and into

the future

- o Maintain a good work/life balance while making enough money to feel safe and comfortable
- o Try to always be kind and supportive to other human beings, even when I disagree with them
- o Leave this world having made it a better place
- My professional goals are…
  - o Help people get unstuck
  - o Work with people I like and believe in, and who like me
  - o Teach people the skills they need to achieve their goals
  - o Write more books and content that makes a difference in the lives of others
  - o Improve the business world by teaching and coaching people to be better communicators

Part 2: My Value and Differentiators

- Who is my audience(s)?
  - People who want to be better leaders
  - People who feel stuck in their careers or businesses
  - People who want to become better speakers and presenters or who fear public speaking
  - Teams who need to understand each other better so they can communicate more effectively
- What problems do I solve for them?
  - Provide an impartial, safe space to discuss issues
  - Help them get unstuck
  - Overcome fear of speaking or presenting
  - Teach presentation skills they were never taught
  - Teach leadership skills they were never taught
  - Make them a better communicator and improve relationships, at work and at home

- What gives me credibility with them?
    - Certified teacher
    - University professor
    - Brand communications expert
    - Experience in both large and small organizations
    - Marketing expert
    - Client testimonials
    - Published works (need more)
    - Successful businessman and entrepreneur
    - Significant studies in communications (2 degrees, and a certificate program)
- What value do I bring to them through my work?
    - I will customize a solution that will get them from point A to point B, likely faster than through other means
    - A varied background that is rooted in communication and relationship building
    - A perspective only I can bring to the table

- o 28 years of real-world experience in a variety of settings (big corporate, small business)
- o Proven track record
- What results will I create for them?
  - o Self-discovery and self-awareness that they never had before
  - o The confidence they need to succeed
  - o Tangible improvement in relationships
  - o A problem solved AND skills and awareness they will carry with them throughout their lifetime
- How do I want them to describe me to their friends, family, and colleagues?
  - o A master communicator
  - o A good person who genuinely cares
  - o Dedicated
  - o Kind
  - o Supportive
  - o Invested
  - o Someone who truly helped me in a time of need
  - o A trusted teacher, coach, and advisor

Part 3: Common Themes or Threads

- Teaching
- Communications
- Helping people be their best selves, find their superpowers, and feel more confident and fulfilled

REFERENCES

1. How to find the person who can help you get ahead at work. *TEDWomen talk by Carla Harris*, 2018. https://www.ted.com/talks/carla_harris_how_to_find_the_person_who_can_help_you_get_ahead_at_work

2. Get Noticed Without Selling Out, with Laura Huang. *Coaching for Leaders* podcast. https://coachingforleaders.com/podcast/get-noticed-laura-huang/

ABOUT THE AUTHOR

Michael Piperno is a leadership communication expert and coach who helps individuals and teams communicate clearly, speak and present effectively, build and maintain positive and healthy business relationships, and lead with confidence. His coaching methodology is the culmination of 3 decades of experience as an actor, educator, writer, communication strategist, and senior executive.

Michael specializes in helping mid- to senior-level talent improve their communication skills and refine their personal brands, so they can improve their effectiveness as leaders and achieve their personal and professional goals. Having changed careers 4 times, he is also a career transition expert who has helped many clients find their purpose and clearly define the next chapter of their careers. In addition, Michael is a skilled advisor to teams with communication problems that impact internal dynamics and corporate culture, and to entrepreneurs who want to position their companies for success.

Michael holds a Master of Science in strategic communication from Purdue University and bachelor's degrees in communication studies and speech and theatre arts from Montclair State University.
His communication strategy work has been recognized by the Global Awards for Healthcare Communications; the Medical, Marketing & Media (MM&M) awards; the Davey Awards; and the Communicator Awards.

Learn more at MichaelPiperno.com or WeAreComvia.com

Made in the USA
Monee, IL
03 June 2023